A MAN OF HONOR

THE ADVENTURES OF KRISTOS KAPATOS

ELENI KAPATOU

Prime Seven Media
518 Landmann St.
Tomah City, WI 54660

Printed in the United States of America

Dedication

To my beloved father, Christos Kapatos —

A man who taught me that true strength lies not in power, but in love, sacrifice, and honor.

You faced storms on the sea and storms in life with unshakable dignity.

This book is for you — so that your story will sail on forever in the hearts of all who read it.

And to all those who carry their families through life's storms — silently, faithfully, humbly — this is for you, too.

And above all, this book is also for the young children —

those who may not yet understand the sacrifices of their fathers, but one day will.

May it help close the distance between generations and shine light on the quiet courage that lives in the hearts of those who love us deeply.

— Elena Kapatou

Table of Contents

"Father, My Hero"

Father, my hero, you are the diamond of the world,
Son of the sea and the pride of God.
My beloved father, my heroic father,
A man who has traveled the world.

I traveled to the other side of the earth
And found my destination,
But I still long for your guidance.

I returned, kneeling, before the monument of a hero
And wept like a child,
Just as I did when I was born for you.
I broke down, I laid a wreath—
A wreath for heroes.

I fought against the thorns
that surrounded your resting place.
My hands bled, I was wounded.
I fought like a soldier,
Faithful to my duty and the Fifth Commandment.
It was the day of the Holy Spirit.

Father, my hero, you are the diamond of the world,
Son of the sea and the pride of God.

My brave father, my noble flower,
Crowned with laurel,
The pride of our ancestors and my beloved one.

Father, I was filled with fury—I will bring a storm.
Father, give me strength—I will bring a Presence.

My beloved father,
Your daughter, Eleni.

Foreward

Bridging Generations Through a Story of Honor

There are people whose lives seem larger than life—people who sail through unimaginable storms and yet remain steady, calm, and strong for those around them.

My father, Christos Kapatos, was one of those people.

He was a Master Captain who traveled across the oceans of the world, but his greatest voyages were not only on ships—they were within the heart of family, love, and sacrifice.

Growing up, I knew him not only as a man of the sea but as a man of silence, dignity, and depth.

A man who would risk his life to protect others, who would endure unimaginable hardship without ever asking for anything in return.

As I became an adult, I started hearing stories from sailors, from family, from friends—stories that painted the full picture of the man my father was:

The Captain who faced storms, fires, and near-sinking ships.

The man who survived an attack that almost took his life, only to fight harder for his family.

The father who loved poetry, who quoted Kavafis as though the words were part of his own soul.

This book is my attempt to honor that story.

A Book for Fathers, Sons, and Daughters

But this book is not just about my father.

It is for every child who has ever looked up to their father and tried to understand his sacrifices.

It is for every father who has carried burdens in silence, never explaining the weight he carries to his children.

In today's world, where so many young children feel disconnected from their fathers, where the gap between generations grows wider, this book seeks to minimize that distance.

I hope that in reading my father's journey, young people will see their own fathers differently—not just as providers, but as men who, in their own way, have battled life's storms for their families.

And I hope fathers who read this will see that sharing their struggles with their children is not a sign of weakness, but a bridge that brings hearts closer together.

This book is my way of keeping my father's memory alive. But it is also a love letter to all fathers and children—to the unspoken bond that exists between them, to the moments that may never be fully understood until it is too late.

A Story That Lives Beyond These Pages

I wrote this book not only for him, but for everyone who seeks to understand what true honor looks like.

To share with the world the life of a man of honor—whose example teaches us that courage is not about never being afraid, but about loving something—someone—so much that you face every fear to protect them.

I hope as you read this story, you will not only see the life of my father but also find reflections of your own fathers, mothers, brothers, and sisters—those who have fought quietly to keep us safe, who have sailed through life's roughest seas without complaint.

This book is for him—but it is also for you, the reader, so that his lessons of love, sacrifice, and honor can live on.

— Eleni Kapatou

Acknowledgement

This book would not have been possible without the love,
support, and memories shared by those who knew my father.

To my family — thank you for keeping his memory
alive in your hearts, for sharing your stories, and for
reminding me every day of the man he was.

To my mother — for your strength during the hardest
times, for loving him through every storm, and for
teaching us what quiet heroism looks like.

To my siblings — for walking beside me on this journey
of remembering and honoring our father.

To the sailors and friends who served under him, who still speak of
him with respect and admiration — **thank you for seeing the man
he was, for standing by him, and for sharing his story with me.**

To all those who believe in living with honor, courage, and love
— **thank you for carrying the same values my father lived by.**

And to the young children —
those who may one day read this story and see in it a reflection
of their own father, grandfather, or even their future self:
This story is also for you.

May it help you understand the strength behind quiet love, the meaning of sacrifice, and the power of a life lived with honor.

And finally, to my father —
Thank you for being my anchor in this life.
Your lessons are the wind in my sails.
You are forever in my heart.

About the Author

Eleni Kapatou is the daughter of Christos Kapatos, the man whose life of courage, love, and honor inspired this book.

Raised in a family shaped by her father's strength and sacrifices, Eleni has carried his values into her own life and career. With a deep respect for her family's maritime history, she has chosen to share her father's story as a way of preserving his legacy and offering inspiration to others who seek examples of true courage in everyday life.

She lives with her own family, continuing to honor her father's memory by living with integrity, compassion, and quiet strength — just as he taught her.

CHAPTER 1

The Birth of Christos – A Legacy Begins

T he town of Messolongi was a place where the sky met the sea in a quiet embrace, a land of fishermen, poets, and warriors. The salty breeze carried stories of history—tales of freedom, resilience, and sacrifice. It was here, on August 15, 1964, that Christos Kapatos was born. His arrival was not just another birth in this coastal town; it was the continuation of a family's long and tested journey.

A Family Forged in War

Long before Christos was born, the Kapatos family had already been shaped by war. His father, Dionysios Kapatos, was born on the island of Kefalonia, a place known for its breathtaking beauty and tragic wartime history. In 1940, when World War II erupted across Europe, Greece was drawn into the conflict. Dionysios, like many young Greek men, was caught in the storm.

At just nineteen years old, Dionysios was forced to leave his home and relocate to Messolongi as the war spread across the Ionian Islands.

In 1941, after Greece was occupied by Axis forces—Nazi Germany, Fascist Italy, and Bulgaria, life became a daily battle for survival.

The Ionian Islands, including Kefalonia, suffered greatly during the occupation. In September 1943, after Italy surrendered to the Allies, German forces retaliated with one of the war's most brutal massacres—the Cephalonia Massacre. The German army executed thousands of Italian soldiers from the Acqui Division who had refused to surrender. The bloodshed was so devastating that Kefalonia became a symbol of wartime cruelty.

Dionysios had already started a new life in Messolongi by then, but war still found its way into his home. His older sons from his first marriage joined the resistance, fighting against the Italian and German occupiers. Their bravery earned them distinction, but at a great cost.

A Family of Heroes

Among Christos' older half-brothers, one stood out—a man whose courage would earn him a place in history. During the war, he fought bravely in the mountains of Epirus and Central Greece, resisting the Axis occupation. In one of the final battles before Greece's liberation in 1944, he was gravely wounded. His injuries left him permanently disabled, but his sacrifice was not forgotten.

After the war ended, the Greek government recognized him as a war hero, awarding him medals for valor and sacrifice. His name was inscribed among the nation's honored soldiers, and though his body bore the scars of war, his spirit remained unbroken.

For Christos, growing up in the shadow of such stories meant that heroism and sacrifice were not just history—they were family legacy. He was raised with the echoes of war still lingering in his home, with the knowledge that survival was not a right but something earned through strength, honor, and resilience.

Anecdote: The Soldier's Coat

One cold winter night, when Christos was just six years old, his mother Eleni took him to visit his war-hero older brother. The house smelled of burning wood and strong Greek coffee, a small sanctuary from the bitter wind outside.

Christos sat quietly, watching his brother—his strong hands now marked with age and hardship, his once-powerful legs now struggling under the weight of war's consequences.

Noticing the boy's silence, the old soldier smiled and reached behind his chair, pulling out a faded military coat, its once-proud insignias now worn with time.

"Do you know what this is, Christo?" he asked, his voice deep and steady.

Christos shook his head.

"This coat kept me alive in the mountains. It was torn, burned, and soaked in rain, but it never left my back. I lost friends, I lost my health, but I kept going because of something greater than myself. Do you know what that was?"

Christos thought for a moment, then shrugged.

His brother leaned forward, his eyes sharp despite the years. *"Duty. Honor. Family."* He placed the coat in Christos' hands, the heavy wool rough against the boy's fingers. *"One day, you will carry your own battles, Christo. And when that day comes, remember—never let go of your duty, your honor, or your family."*

The words stayed with him. Long after his brother passed, long after he left Messolongi, Christos would remember that coat and what it stood for.

Loss and Hardship

Though the war had ended, its effects never truly disappeared. Dionysios, carrying the weight of war and loss, tried to build a new life in Messolongi. He married his first wife, had three children, and for a time, found peace. But fate had its own plans.

His first wife passed away young, leaving behind three orphaned children. Alone and burdened by responsibility, Dionysios remarried, hoping to rebuild what he had lost. His second wife, Eleni, was a woman of strength and resilience, known for her work as a practical doctor, tending to the ill with skill and compassion. Together, they had three children—the last of whom was Christos.

From the beginning, Christos' birth carried weight. He was not just another son; he was the youngest, the final link in a chain of hardships, hopes, and endurance.

Yet, life had other plans. When Christos was just eight years old, his father passed away, leaving him and his family in sudden darkness.

A child no longer, Christos was forced to become a man before his time.

Key Lessons from Chapter 1

1. **War Leaves a Lasting Impact**

    Christos grew up hearing stories of courage, loss, and sacrifice from WWII. The scars of war didn't fade with time—they shaped his family's values and resilience.

2. **Heroism Runs in Families**

    His older half-brother's bravery in WWII, which earned him the title of a disabled war hero, showed Christos that honor and sacrifice define a person's legacy.

3. **Hardship Can Shape You, But It Doesn't Define You**

    Christos faced adversity from a young age, but he did not allow it to break him. Instead, it fueled his determination to rise above his circumstances.

4. **The Power of a Single Lesson**

    The story of the soldier's coat left an impression on Christos. It was a reminder that, no matter the hardship, duty, honor, and family must always come first.

5. **Dreams Are Born in the Struggle**

Despite financial hardship and the weight of responsibility, Christos dared to dream beyond the rice fields of Messolongi. His vision of a bigger future began when he refused to accept limitations.

6. **The Sea is a Metaphor for Life**

Just as the sea is vast and unpredictable, so is life. Christos understood early on that life would take him beyond his small town, but he would need courage to sail into the unknown.

CHAPTER 2

The Boy Who Dreamed of the Sea

M essolongi was a town of quiet resilience, its people shaped by the salt air, the ever-changing tides, and the weight of history. For Christos Kapatos, childhood was not a time of innocence, but of responsibility. While other boys played in the narrow streets or swam in the warm waters of the Gulf, Christos worked.

By the time he was eight years old, he had already learned what it meant to labor under the hot Greek sun. His father's death had left a void—not just emotional, but economic. His mother, Eleni, did her best to keep the family afloat with her work as a practical doctor, but there was never quite enough.

So, Christos did what was necessary.

At dawn, while the town still slept, he walked to the rice fields, his bare feet sinking into the damp soil. The work was exhausting, his small hands struggling to keep up with the men around him. But he never complained. He listened. He observed. And most of all, he dreamed.

A Role Model in the Neighborhood

Even as a child, Christos had a presence that commanded respect. The younger boys in the neighborhood looked up to him—not just because he was strong or hardworking, but because he carried himself with a quiet confidence and integrity beyond his years.

To them, Christos was the standard.

They watched how he balanced his studies with work, how he spoke politely to elders, and how he never backed down from a challenge. They saw him run faster, swim farther, and stand taller than anyone else they knew. He was the boy they all wanted to be.

One evening, a group of younger children gathered around him after he returned from the rice fields.

"Christos, how do you work all day and still have energy to study?" one boy asked in awe.

Christos smiled, wiping the sweat from his forehead. *"Because I have a goal. If you know where you're going, you don't feel tired. You just keep moving."*

The words stayed with them. Long after he left for Athens, the children of Messolongi would tell stories about Christos, the boy who never gave up.

Many years later, one of those children, Mr. Christos, would follow in his footsteps.

A Legacy Remembered

Decades later, Christos' first daughter, Eleni, chose the same path as her father, entering the maritime industry. One day, while working, she met a man who had grown up in Messolongi—Mr. Christos, one of the small boys who had once idolized her father.

Upon hearing her last name, his face lit up with recognition and admiration.

"Are you Christos Kapatos' daughter?" he asked.

"Yes," Eleni replied, intrigued.

The man smiled with pride. *"Your father was my hero. As kids, we all wanted to be like him. He was strong, smart, and never gave up. He inspired me to become a captain. I wouldn't be here today without his example."*

Eleni felt a wave of pride and emotion wash over her. Her father's legacy wasn't just in books or memories—it lived on in the people he had influenced.

That day, she understood something powerful: her father had not just built a career—he had built a legacy.

The Struggle to Leave Messolongi

By the time Christos reached nineteen, he had come to a crossroads. He had completed his schooling, but the small town could no longer contain his ambitions. He had to decide: stay and build a quiet life, or chase the unknown?

The answer came unexpectedly—through family.

His older half-sister, the daughter of Dionysios' first marriage, had settled in Athens with her husband. She offered Christos a place to stay if he wished to pursue higher education. The opportunity was too great to ignore.

Her husband, Mr. Giakoumis, was not just any man—he was a former football player for Olympiacos, one of Greece's most prestigious teams. His success had taken him from the playing fields of Greece's most competitive stadiums to a comfortable life in Athens.

When Christos arrived, Giakoumis recognized something familiar in the young man—ambition, hunger, and discipline.

"You remind me of myself when I was young," Giakoumis told him one evening over dinner. *"Talent is nothing without hard work. If you want to achieve something in this world, you must be willing to outwork everyone else."*

Christos listened carefully. Here was a man who had fought his way to success, not with words, but with action. And now, Athens was calling Christos to do the same.

But leaving was not so simple.

His mother, Eleni, was heartbroken at the thought of her youngest son leaving Messolongi.

"*Christos, we have already lost so much. First your father, then your brothers to war. Now you want to go too?*" she asked, her eyes filled with worry.

Christos took her hands in his. "*Mother, I promise I will not forget you. I will take care of you, no matter where I am. But I have to do this. I have to make something of myself.*"

Eleni sighed, knowing she could not hold him back forever. She was proud of her son, but her heart ached at the thought of him leaving.

His siblings also had mixed feelings. Some supported him, knowing he had potential, while others feared he was chasing an uncertain future. But Christos knew—staying in Messolongi would never be enough for him.

With a single bag packed with clothes, books, and hope, Christos boarded a bus to Athens. As he watched the familiar streets of Messolongi fade into the distance, he felt a mix of excitement and sorrow.

Stavros' words echoed in his mind: "*Leave with your heart full, not empty.*"

He wasn't running away—he was running toward something bigger.

Key Lessons from Chapter 2

1. **Hard Work Shapes Character**

   Christos learned from a young age that hard work was not optional—it was survival. Every hour in the rice fields built his resilience and discipline.

2. **Wisdom Comes from Unexpected Places**

   The old fisherman Stavros warned him that life rewards those who chase something bigger than themselves. This lesson would guide Christos throughout his life.

3. **Education Opens Doors**

   Despite his responsibilities, Christos remained dedicated to his studies, proving that knowledge could be the key to escaping hardship.

4. **Sports and Discipline Go Hand in Hand**

   Like his future mentor Giakoumis, Christos understood that athletic discipline translated into life discipline. Strength of body and mind was his greatest asset.

5. **The Right Mentors Make a Difference**

   From his teacher Mr. Papadakis to his brother-in-law Giakoumis, Christos was surrounded by strong role models who shaped his mindset.

6. **Leaving Home is Never Easy**

No matter how big the dream, leaving loved ones behind is painful. Christos had to choose between comfort and ambition—and he chose ambition.

7. **Legacy is Built Through Influence**

Years later, when his daughter Eleni met one of the boys he had inspired, she realized that Christos' influence extended far beyond his own family. He had set a standard that others aspired to reach.

CHAPTER 3

The Captain's Journey Begins

The journey from Messolongi to Athens was more than just a change in location—it was the first step toward a destiny Christos had long envisioned. As the bus rumbled across the rugged Greek landscape, he gazed out at the countryside, reflecting on the sacrifices that had brought him here.

Athens, the capital of Greece, was a city of contradictions—ancient yet modern, chaotic yet full of opportunities. It was a world away from the quiet shores of Messolongi. Here, he would chase his dream of becoming a Master Captain, navigating the vast oceans that had called to him since childhood.

But Christos' journey was not just personal. It was deeply intertwined with the history of his family and the larger historical events that had shaped them all.

The Shadow of War:
A Family Defined by History

Though Christos was born long after the end of World War II, the war had cast a long shadow over his family. His father, Dionysios Kapatos, had been a survivor of that conflict, carrying with him stories of both tragedy and resilience.

Dionysios was born in Kefalonia, a Greek island that had suffered greatly during the war. In 1941, when Greece was occupied by Axis forces (Germany, Italy, and Bulgaria), Kefalonia became a battleground. The Italian and German armies fought for control, leaving the island's people caught in the middle.

By 1943, after Italy's surrender to the Allies, German forces launched one of the war's most brutal massacres—the Massacre of the Acqui Division, where over 5,000 Italian soldiers were executed. Though Dionysios was not a soldier, he witnessed firsthand the destruction of his homeland. The war forced him to leave Kefalonia, and like many others, he sought refuge in the mainland.

At just 19 years old, Dionysios arrived in Messolongi, a town that, despite its struggles, offered safety. It was here that he built a new life, married, and later fathered Christos. But the war had already taken its toll. The hardship, hunger, and suffering of those years remained with him.

The Heroes of War:
Christos' Brothers

Christos' older half-brothers, the children from his father's first marriage, had been distinguished soldiers during World War II.

One of them, a decorated war hero, had been seriously wounded in battle and was recognized as a disabled veteran. His courage and sacrifice were honored by the Greek government, but the scars—both physical and emotional—remained.

Growing up, Christos often heard stories of his brothers' bravery, their struggles on the battlefield, and their unwavering devotion to Greece. Though he had not experienced war himself, he carried their legacy in his heart. Their resilience became his standard for strength.

Athens:
A City of New Beginnings

When Christos arrived in Athens, he was immediately overwhelmed by its sheer size and energy. Unlike Messolongi, where everyone knew each other, Athens was a city of strangers, moving at a relentless pace.

His first stop was his sister's home, where he was greeted with warmth and familiarity. Her husband, Mr. Giakoumis, the former Olympiacos football player, welcomed him with firm advice.

"Athens will test you, Christos. It's not easy, but it will make you stronger. Just like the game of football—you have to stay focused and never lose sight of your goal."

Christos took his words to heart. His goal was clear—to enroll in one of Greece's most prestigious maritime academies: The University of Hydra.

The University of Hydra:
Entering the World of the Sea

The University of Hydra was legendary. Founded to train Greece's next generation of maritime leaders, it had produced some of the finest Master Captains, engineers, and ship operators.

Becoming a Master Captain was not just about commanding a vessel— it was about mastering the art of navigation, leadership, and survival. Christos knew this path would be demanding, but he was ready.

From the first day, he found himself surrounded by ambitious young men, all eager to prove themselves.

One of his professors, Captain Anagnostopoulos, a veteran with over 30 years at sea, addressed the students:

> *"The sea is not for the weak. It will test your patience, your strength, and your will to survive. If you think this is just about steering a ship, you are mistaken. To be a Captain is to be responsible for every life on board, through storms, wars, and the unknown."*

Christos listened intently. This was the kind of challenge he had been waiting for.

Facing Hardships:
The Cost of His Dreams

As expected, the coursework was rigorous. Christos spent long nights studying maritime laws, navigation charts, and mechanical engineering. The practical training was even tougher—weeks at sea, grueling physical endurance tests, and simulations of emergency situations.

At times, he felt exhausted, but he refused to give up.

Yet, the biggest hardship was being away from his family. His mother, Eleni, still struggled with his absence.

In her letters, she often wrote:

> *"My dear Christos, I pray for you every night. I wish you were here, but I know this is your path. Just promise me—you will never forget where you come from."*

Her words kept him grounded. No matter how far he traveled, Messolongi would always be home.

Key Lessons from Chapter 3

1. **History Shapes Us**

   Christos' journey was influenced by his family's past, particularly his father's survival during WWII and his brothers' heroism.

   He carried their legacy of resilience and bravery into his own path.

2. **New Beginnings Require Courage**

    Leaving a small town for a big city was daunting, but Christos knew that comfort never leads to greatness.

3. **Mentors Matter**

    From his brother-in-law Giakoumis to Captain Anagnostopoulos, Christos surrounded himself with wise role models who pushed him to grow.

4. **Mastery Takes Discipline**

    Studying at the University of Hydra was not just about learning to command a ship—it was about becoming a leader under pressure.

5. **Sacrifice is the Price of Success**

    Being away from his mother and siblings was painful, but dreams require difficult choices.

6. **Hardships Prepare Us for Greater Challenges**

    The grueling training at the maritime academy toughened him physically and mentally, preparing him for the real dangers of the sea.

CHAPTER 4

Into the Deep Waters

C hristos Kapatos stood at the bow of the ship, inhaling the salty air as the vessel rocked gently beneath him. The day he had dreamed of had finally arrived—he was no longer a student, no longer bound by the classroom walls of the University of Hydra. He was now a seafarer, stepping into a world of vast oceans, unpredictable storms, and uncharted territories.

But the sea was not just a place of adventure; it was a merciless teacher. Christos had heard the stories—tales of ships lost in storms, of fires breaking out on tankers, of captains forced to make impossible decisions. He knew that the life of a mariner was filled with both glory and danger. And now, it was time to face it for himself.

What he didn't know was that many years later, he would face his own maritime disasters—an accident that nearly sank his ship, a fire on board, and a serious incident in Jeddah, one of the most religious places on Earth. But before those trials, he had to first prove himself on the open sea.

The First Voyage:
Aboard the Merchant Fleet

At age 25, Christos embarked on his first official voyage as a junior officer aboard a Greek-owned merchant ship. The vessel was a chemical tanker, designed to transport hazardous cargo across international waters. It was a high-risk operation—one wrong move, and the chemicals onboard could ignite, leading to catastrophe.

His first assignment took him through some of the world's most treacherous waters. He sailed through the Aegean Sea, the Mediterranean, the Suez Canal, and into the vast Indian Ocean, where storms brewed without warning.

The senior officers tested him from the start.

"You think you know the sea, boy?" the Chief Officer had said on his first day. *"Wait until she gets angry."*

Christos listened more than he spoke, absorbing every bit of knowledge he could from the seasoned sailors around him.

Historical Maritime Events:
The Risks of the Open Sea

As Christos sailed into his new life, the maritime industry was undergoing major transformations, shaped by both disasters and innovation. He was entering the profession at a time when shipping had become the lifeblood of global trade, but also one of its most dangerous industries.

1. The Tragedy of the SS Heraklion (1966)

Though it had happened years before his time at sea, the story of the SS Heraklion was well-known among Greek sailors. The ferry, traveling from Crete to Piraeus, sank during a fierce storm in the Aegean Sea, taking more than 200 lives.

Sailors whispered about it in the mess halls, sharing tales of what went wrong—poorly secured cargo, an overloaded ship, and a captain who had trusted the weather too much.

For Christos, it was a chilling reminder: the sea did not forgive mistakes.

2. The Sinking of the Amoco Cadiz (1978)

While Christos was still early in his career, the Amoco Cadiz, a massive oil tanker, ran aground off the coast of France, spilling over 220,000 tons of crude oil into the ocean.

This event sparked global changes in maritime safety, leading to stricter environmental laws and better ship designs. Christos followed these changes closely, realizing that his career would not just be about navigating waters—but navigating an evolving industry.

3. The MV Derbyshire (1980) – A Lesson in Strength

A few years after Christos began his career, the MV Derbyshire, a British bulk carrier, mysteriously vanished during a typhoon in the Pacific Ocean. The entire 44-man crew perished, making it one of the greatest shipping disasters of the time.

Investigations later revealed structural weaknesses in the ship's design—proof that even the largest vessels could be fragile in the face of nature.

These disasters reinforced a harsh reality for Christos: a captain's job was not just to sail—but to safeguard every soul on board.

The Test:
A Storm in the Indian Ocean

It didn't take long for Christos to face his own trial at sea.

One night, as they crossed the Indian Ocean, a cyclone formed unexpectedly, with winds reaching 150 km/h (93 mph). The ship lurched violently, throwing crew members against the walls. The waves rose as high as buildings, crashing over the deck and flooding parts of the ship.

Christos, still a junior officer, was on duty when the call came from the bridge.

"Secure the cargo! Check the ballast tanks!" the captain barked.

Amid the chaos, Christos moved swiftly, ensuring that every chemical container was locked in place. He had read about the Titanic disaster—how poor structural integrity had doomed a mighty ship. He refused to let history repeat itself on his watch.

For 12 straight hours, the crew battled the storm. At one point, Christos saw a deckhand slip on the wet metal floor, nearly being swept overboard. Without hesitation, he lunged forward, grabbing the man's collar and pulling him to safety.

By morning, the storm had passed. The ship, though battered, had survived.

The captain, an old, grizzled man, placed a firm hand on Christos' shoulder.

"You kept your head when others panicked," he said. "You'll make a fine captain one day."

Those words stayed with Christos. He wasn't just surviving the sea— he was mastering it.

Foreshadowing:
The Future Trials Awaiting Him

Years later, Christos would face far greater dangers.

A near-sinking accident would push his skills to the limit, testing every bit of knowledge and courage he had gained over the years.

A fire on board would force him to act swiftly, knowing that fire was the deadliest enemy on a tanker carrying hazardous cargo.

In Jeddah, Saudi Arabia, a serious accident would unfold in the most religiously significant and culturally strict place on Earth, requiring not just maritime expertise but also diplomatic wisdom.

These trials would define him not just as a sailor, but as a leader.

Key Lessons from Chapter 4

1. **The Sea is Unforgiving**

    The disasters of the SS Heraklion, Amoco Cadiz, and MV Derbyshire showed Christos that even the strongest ships could fall. Respect for the ocean was the first rule of survival.

2. **Adaptation is Key**

    With new maritime regulations emerging after disasters, Christos learned that a good captain must always evolve, keeping up with safety measures, technology, and industry changes.

3. **Leadership is Built in Crisis**

    During the Indian Ocean storm, Christos proved that a captain is not just measured by his skills—but by his courage under pressure.

4. **A Captain Protects His Crew**

    Saving the deckhand from being swept overboard reminded him: leadership is about protecting those who follow you, even in the face of danger.

5. **The Sea Never Stops Testing You**

    The near-sinking, the fire, and the Jeddah accident were yet to come, but even early in his career, Christos knew that the ocean would never stop challenging him.

Next Chapter: The Call of Australia

In Chapter 5, Christos' journey takes a dramatic turn when he reaches Melbourne, Australia. A routine port call leads to an unexpected opportunity that will change his life forever.

Next Chapter: Into the Deep Waters

In Chapter 4, Christos graduates from the University of Hydra and embarks on his first sea voyage. He faces the unpredictable dangers of the ocean, navigates his first storms, and learns that being a Captain is more than just knowing how to sail—it's about leading men, making split-second decisions, and surviving against all odds.

CHAPTER 5

The Call of Australia

When Christos Kapatos first arrived in Melbourne, Australia, he was greeted by a world that was completely unlike his beloved Messolongi—modern, fast-moving, alive with energy, but also warm with the voices of Greeks who had made this land their home. What was supposed to be a brief stay as part of his ship's journey unexpectedly became a chapter that would forever divide his heart.

A City of Promise and a Familiar Tongue

Melbourne's Greek community embraced Christos as one of their own. His uncles, cousins, and old family friends surrounded him, offering him a home, support, and even a future.

"You don't need to return to the sea, Christos," one uncle said as they sat around a table filled with grilled lamb, feta, olives, and wine. "Look around you—so many Greeks have built their lives here. You are smart, strong. You can have a home, a family, and never fear the waves again."

For a moment, Christos let himself imagine that future—a house in a quiet suburb, children running in the yard, dinners with family.

A New Life, a Divided Soul

With the help of his relatives, Christos quickly found work in real estate, a field that allowed him to use his sharp mind, discipline, and natural charm. Soon, he was enrolling in studies at the University of Melbourne, becoming a professional real estate broker.

People trusted him. Within months, Greek families buying their first homes turned to Christos for help. His reputation grew: the captain who had traded the sea for success on land.

But while his days were filled with business meetings and clients, his nights were heavy with longing.

When he returned home each evening, sitting on the veranda under the vast Australian sky, he thought of the quiet beaches of Messolongi, the sea breeze that never left him, and his mother Eleni, sitting alone by the window, waiting.

"What am I doing here?" he would wonder, staring into the darkness, his heart torn between two worlds.

The Love That Couldn't Keep Him

In Melbourne, Christos met an Australian woman, kind and full of life. For a time, she brought joy to his lonely heart. They dreamed aloud of a life together: a house, a family, perhaps even a return trip to Greece someday.

But as their love deepened, so did Christos' inner struggle.

"Christos, stay with me," she said one night, as they walked along the Yarra River, city lights twinkling around them. "You don't have to go back. We can have everything here."

He took her hands in his.

"My heart is not only here. Part of me is out there," he said, gesturing toward the ocean. "I belong to the sea. I belong to Greece. And I belong to my mother, who waits for me."

Her eyes filled with tears. "Then there's nothing I can do to make you stay?"

"If I stay," Christos whispered, "I lose myself."

And so, with a heavy heart, he left Australia, knowing that he was walking away from love, comfort, and the life he had built.

Returning to Messolongi:
The Regret That Hit Like a Wave

The moment Christos set foot in Messolongi, his heart sank.

What he had dreamed about in Australia—the town he had missed, the comfort of home—felt strangely distant and small now. The streets seemed narrower, the faces older. Friends had moved on, and life in Messolongi had stood still.

"Is this what I longed for?" he thought, walking through the dusty streets, past the houses that hadn't changed since he was a boy.

The quietness of the town, once a refuge, now felt like a prison.

And when he saw his mother Eleni, her eyes filled with joy and tears, Christos felt a wave of guilt and sorrow.

"You are home, Christos," she whispered, embracing him tightly. "You're home."

But he couldn't bring himself to share his regret—how he had left a life behind, left a woman he loved, left a part of himself in Australia.

As the days passed, Christos grew restless.

He would walk to the edge of town, to the shoreline where he had played as a boy, staring at the sea and feeling like a bird trapped in a cage.

"I thought coming home would bring peace," he whispered to himself, watching the waves. "But my soul belongs out there."

Caught Between Two Worlds

Christos realized that his homesickness in Australia had been for Greece, but now, back in Greece, he was homesick for something else—his freedom, his life at sea, and perhaps even the love he had left behind.

He had become a man caught between two worlds, belonging fully to neither.

But one thing was certain: the sea was calling him back.

Foreshadowing the Future

Christos would not remain long on land. Soon, he would return to the ships and the life of a sailor, this time as a Master Captain, facing challenges that would test his courage, wisdom, and leadership:

A near-sinking event, where only his calm and skill would prevent disaster.

A fire on board, where he would fight not just for the ship, but for the lives of his crew.

A dangerous incident in Jeddah, where cultural and religious tensions would require diplomacy and strength.

Key Lessons from Chapter 5

1. **The Past We Long For May Not Be What We Imagine**

Christos learned that sometimes, when we return home, we find a place that no longer fits us.

2. **A Divided Heart Can Never Rest**

His heart was torn between love, family, and destiny—and no easy answer could heal that pain.

3. **Destiny is a Calling You Cannot Deny**

No matter how far Christos tried to run, the sea was his destiny, and it would always call him back.

4. **Regret is Part of Choosing the Hard Path**

By returning home, Christos gained peace with his family but lost a life he had built abroad—a price he would carry quietly.

5. **We Belong Where Our Purpose Lives**

In the end, his true home was not a place, but the life he was born to live—on the sea.

CHAPTER 6

The Master of the Sea Rises

(Expanded with Letters to His Mother)

Leaving Messolongi for the sea once again was a painful choice, but Christos Kapatos knew his destiny lay beyond the shore. Though his mother Eleni held him tightly at the port, her eyes filled with tears, Christos' heart was torn.

"You have to go, don't you, my son?" she asked, knowing the answer long before he spoke.

"Yes, mother. But I promise you, I'll write. I'll write to you as often as I can."

And he did.

A Captain Who Never Forgot His Mother

Though Christos sailed across the world—through storms, fires, and dangers unknown—his thoughts always returned to Messolongi and to his mother waiting by the window.

From every port he reached, every country where he docked, Christos wrote letters to his beloved Eleni—long, detailed letters filled with descriptions of his voyages, his crew, and even his quiet moments of reflection.

"My dearest mother," he would begin. "Today we reached the port of Rotterdam. The sea was wild for many days, but now we are safe. Do not worry for me. I always think of you when I see the calm after a storm. It reminds me of your gentle strength."

Sometimes, he would include pressed flowers or small trinkets from distant lands, tokens to remind her that no matter how far he traveled, he was still her son.

"I saw a market today in Istanbul, mother, and it reminded me of our old market days in Messolongi. How I miss those mornings with you."

His letters became her lifeline—words that gave her peace, knowing her son was alive and thinking of her. And for Christos, writing to his mother was a way to stay grounded, to hold on to love and home in a world that was often lonely and dangerous.

From Officer to Master Captain — The Journey of Leadership

Christos rose through the ranks, his reputation growing with every voyage. No longer a junior officer, he became Master Captain, commanding massive chemical tankers and LPG vessels that sailed across oceans carrying dangerous cargo.

But no matter how high he rose, his letters to his mother continued.

"Mother, today we passed through the Suez Canal. The desert stretched endlessly on both sides, but my thoughts are always of home, of you waiting in Messolongi. The sea is wide, but your love reaches me even here."

Trials on the Open Sea — Testing the Master

The First Great Storm

As Master Captain, Christos faced his first deadly storm in the South China Sea.

Waves like monsters from the deep rose against the ship, winds howled with fury, and his crew looked to him with fear.

"Captain, we won't survive this!" one young sailor cried.

But Christos, calm and resolute, gave firm orders:

"Hold steady. Trust the ship, and trust me."

Through twenty hours of relentless battle against nature, Christos' hands never left the wheel, and he guided them to safety.

Later, exhausted and soaked to the bone, he sat in his cabin and wrote to his mother:

"Today, mother, I thought I would not see the sunrise. But God was with us, and I thought of you as I fought that storm. Your strength carried me through."

The Near-Sinking Incident

Years later, a mechanical failure and violent weather left his ship near-sinking, water flooding into the hold. His chemical cargo was at risk of igniting if touched by seawater.

But Christos remained calm. For 14 hours, he led the battle to save the ship, organizing the crew, pumping water, sealing breaches.

When the ship was finally safe, he sat down and wrote again to Eleni:

"Dearest mother, tonight we survived what I hope never to face again. I feared for my men, but we are safe now. I thought of you with every decision I made. I wish I could sit with you now and tell you all, but for now, these words must do."

Fire On Board

On another voyage, a fire broke out—a nightmare on a chemical tanker. But Christos organized the response, fighting the fire with courage and calm leadership, and saved his crew from disaster.

"Mother, today we fought flames that could have taken us all. But as always, I thought of you, and that gave me the strength to lead."

Jeddah:

A Diplomatic Challenge Beyond the Sea

In Jeddah, Saudi Arabia, one of his crew unknowingly violated strict religious customs, putting the whole team at risk of arrest.

Christos had to act as both captain and diplomat, navigating tense negotiations with local authorities, showing deep respect for culture while protecting his crew.

When he later wrote to his mother, he said:

> "Today, I was reminded that the dangers of the sea are not always from storms. Sometimes they are from people and laws we do not fully understand. But I led them safely, mother. As I promised you, I always try to return them all home."

A Son's Love Across Oceans

For Eleni, these letters were treasures. She kept them in a small wooden box by her bedside, and when Christos was away, she would read them over and over, praying for his safety.

Sometimes she would reply, writing in her careful hand:

> "My dear son, I wait for you. Every day I pray to see you again.
> Be careful, Christo mou. Your mother loves you more than
> anything in this world."

Their letters were a bridge between two hearts, spanning oceans,
storms, and years.

Key Lessons from Chapter 6 (Updated)

1. **A Leader Remembers His Roots**

   Christos never forgot his mother and home, writing to Eleni from
   every corner of the world.

2. **Courage Comes from Love**

   His bravery was fueled by his mother's love and the hope of seeing
   home again.

3. **Leadership is Responsibility for Others' Lives**

   Whether facing storms, fire, or diplomatic crises, Christos led
   with honor and calm.

4. **The Sea Takes, But Also Give.**

   Though the sea took him far, it also gave him strength, identity,
   and purpose.

5. **Family Bonds Survive Distance**

Their letters remind us that love can travel across oceans, keeping families close even when separated by the vastest distances.

Next Chapter: The Man Beyond the Captain
— Family, Legacy, and Reflections

In Chapter 7, we will explore Christos' life beyond the
sea—his family, children, and the wisdom he passed
on as a man of honor, courage, and humility.

Chapter 7 under paragraph "family life in Athens" we will add:

Chapter 7 in full, with all the integrated elements — including the
birth of Eleni, Christos' near-death experience, the crying baby, the
mother's struggle, the Jeddah hostage crisis and daring escape, the
family's life in Athens, and the national recognition.

The Man Beyond the Captain — Family, Legacy, and Final Reflections

T hough Christos Kapatos was known across the oceans as a Master Captain, a man of strength and courage, at home he was something far greater — a father, a husband, a man of deep honor whose real heroism began within his own family.

The Birth of a Daughter and the Tragedy That Followed

When his first daughter, Eleni, was born, Christos was filled with joy and pride. He held her gently in his strong arms and whispered promises of protection and love.

But fate was cruel. Just days after her birth, a violent attack by a neighbor — rooted in an old family conflict between their mothers — left Christos fighting for his life, stabbed in the lung.

While Christos lay unconscious in the hospital, his wife was left alone at home with their newborn daughter, struggling to keep her world from falling apart.

The Cry of a Baby Who Felt Her Father's Absence

From that moment, baby Eleni began to cry endlessly, day and night, as if she could sense that her father was gone.

No matter how her mother held her, walked her, or sang to her, the baby's cries filled the apartment like a painful echo of the tragedy.

Neighbors began whispering, worried and confused:

"The baby cries all night. Something is wrong in that house."

A Mother's Desperation — Calling the Doctor

In total despair, Christos' wife called a doctor, hoping there was something that could be done to help her baby.

After examining Eleni, the doctor gently explained:

"Madam, your baby isn't sick. She's crying because she feels everything around her. She knows her father is gone, and she feels your fear."

Though he offered a light medication to help the baby rest, the real cure — her father's return — was far from certain.

The Police Come — A Misunderstood Cry for Help

As the days and nights passed with Eleni's endless crying, neighbors called the police, fearing for the child.

When officers arrived, they found a young mother, pale and exhausted, holding her baby tightly in her arms, surrounded by sorrow.

With tears in her eyes, she told them:

> "My husband is in the hospital. They tried to kill him. My baby cries because she misses him, because she feels my pain."

The police left quietly, realizing they had stepped into a family tragedy deeper than they had imagined.

Christos' Vow — A Father Who Would Live for His Family

When Christos finally awoke and learned what had happened — his wife's suffering, his baby's cries, the police being called — his heart broke more deeply than his body ever could.

He swore quietly to himself:

"As long as I live, I will protect them. They will never be alone again."

Two Years of Staying Ashore — Choosing Family Over Career

Though the sea called him back, Christos delayed returning to his career for two years, determined to stay by his family's side.

He wanted to ensure Eleni was strong enough to stand, to speak, to live without fear.

He wanted his wife to feel safe, to know she was not alone.

"The sea can wait," he said. "But my family cannot."

Family Life in Athens — Preparing for the Future

Eventually, when Eleni grew older and started university, the family moved to Athens to be near her, supporting her studies and building a new chapter of life.

Christos, proud of his daughter's education, would say:

"My Eleni will do great things. She will be stronger than me."

The Jeddah Crisis — A Captain's Greatest Test

But Christos' life at sea was far from over.

Years later, while his family lived in Athens, Christos faced one of the most terrifying challenges of his career when his vessel and crew were held hostage in Jeddah, Saudi Arabia, for over a month, trapped in port due to a dispute between the company and port authorities over unpaid fees.

With no food, no fuel, no supplies, and no solution from his company, Christos watched his men grow weaker by the day.

A Daring Escape — Choosing Action Over Fear

When it became clear no help was coming, Christos made a dangerous decision:

> "If no one will save us, I will. I will get my men home."

With barely enough fuel, Christos secretly moved the ship out of port under the cover of night — risking arrest, prison, and even death.

But he didn't stop there.

Because they lacked fuel, Christos used his mastery of the sea to navigate along natural currents and streams, guiding the vessel like a sailboat, carried by the sea itself toward Greece.

Sailing with the Sea's Help — A Captain Who Knew Her Secrets

His crew watched in awe as Christos read the water, following every shift in current, every breath of wind.

"The sea will help us if we respect her," Christos said. "We'll follow her home."

The Homecoming — A Nation Watches in Awe

When the ship finally reached Piraeus, the story exploded across Greece.

Newspapers everywhere carried Christos' photo in his Master's uniform on their front pages.

"Captain of Honor: Christos Kapatos Saves His Crew from Jeddah."
"Greek Hero Returns — A Modern Odyssey on the High Seas."
"With Wisdom and Courage: A Captain Brings His Men Home."

In Athens, his family wept with joy and pride, seeing his photo everywhere.

Eleni, now a university student, remembers standing still in the street, seeing her father's face on the front page, whispering:

"That's my baba. He made it. He's alive."

A Family's Private Hero

Though Greece celebrated him as a national hero, to his wife and children, Christos was simply the man who never gave up on them, who fought for his family even when the world didn't see.

Final Reflections — The Legacy of Christos Kapatos

Christos Kapatos was not only a great Master Captain, but a man who carried honor, love, and sacrifice in everything he did.

His daughter Eleni would later say:

> "He was a hero to Greece. But to me, he was the man who lived for us, who fought for us, who loved us first. That is the man I will always remember."

Key Lessons from Chapter 7: A Legacy of Love and Honor

1. **A True Hero Protects His Family First**

— Christos delayed his return to sea to stay with his wife and daughter when they needed him most.

2. **A Captain's Duty Is to His Crew and Their Lives, Not Just Orders**

    — In Jeddah, Christos risked everything to save his men.

3. **Strength is Shown in the Quiet Battles at Home**

    — His wife's struggle alone with their crying baby was a battle of love.

4. **The Sea is a Partner to the Wise**

    — Christos' mastery of the sea saved them when no fuel could.

5. **Honor Lives Beyond the Storms**

    — Christos' legacy lives in his family and in all who knew of his courage and love.

The Enduring Memory of a Man of Honor

E pilogue, reflecting on how Christos is remembered today by his family, sailors, and all who knew him — and how his spirit lives on.

Choosing Forgiveness
— Teaching His Children Love Over Hate

Though he carried the scar on his back forever, Christos never let anger take root in his heart.

"I will not raise my children in hate," he said to his wife. "They will grow up knowing love, knowing honor—not bitterness."

His children grew up watching their father choose forgiveness when others would have chosen revenge—a lesson that marked them deeply and shaped their own lives.

A House Filled with Stories, Love, and Poetry

Christos' home was not only filled with love but also with words—stories of the sea, wisdom, and, above all, poetry.

Eleni would always remember her father's love for poetry, especially the works of Constantine Kavafis, whose words spoke of life's journey, dignity, and facing destiny with courage.

"As you set out for Ithaca, hope your road is a long one, full of adventure, full of discovery," Christos would often quote, almost as if Kavafis had written for him.

Sometimes, when Eleni would return from work, tired from the day, she would pause on the stairs outside their home, and from inside, she could hear her father reciting Kavafis in his low, strong voice, as though speaking to the walls, to himself, to life itself.

"When you set out on your journey to Ithaca,
pray that the road is long, full of adventure, full of knowledge."

"I used to stand there, not wanting to interrupt him," Eleni remembers. "It felt like listening to the heart of the house beating."

To Christos, poetry was more than words—it was a way to understand life's storms, to find meaning in the struggle.

A Quiet Man of Deep Emotion

Though Christos was not a man to speak of emotions openly, his love was shown in a thousand small ways:

Fixing things around the house quietly, so no one would worry.

Walking beside his children, teaching them dignity without words.

Holding their hands when they were small, and later, holding their gaze with pride as they grew.

He taught them to respect all people, to never bow their heads out of fear, and to keep their honor intact even when life was hard.

"If you lose everything, but keep your honor, you are still rich," he would say.

Legacy: A Man Who Lived with Dignity, Courage, and Heart

To those who knew him, Christos was more than a captain:

He was a man of rare honor.

A father who led with love and quiet strength.

A husband who carried the weight of danger to give his family a better life.

A friend who never broke his word.

Among sailors, he was remembered as the captain who stood like a mountain in every storm.

Among family, as the man who loved poetry and recited Kavafis like prayers.

Epilogue: The Enduring Memory of a Man of Honor

Years have passed since Christos Kapatos sailed his final voyage, but his story continues to live on — in the hearts of his family, in the stories told by sailors, and in the memory of all who knew what kind of man he was.

Christos Kapatos died suddenly and tragically on August 28, 2018, in a train accident that took him from this world without warning.

Although he had survived the dangers of the sea, fires, near-sinking ships, a violent attack, and even the Jeddah hostage crisis, fate claimed him in an instant, on a day like any other.

The Tragedy that Took Him
— A Life Cut Short

Christos, who had always faced every challenge with strength, collapsed and fired suddenly while on a train, in an accident that shocked everyone who knew him.

It was a moment that no one expected — not for a man who had lived through storms that would have broken anyone else.

"After everything he had survived, to lose him that way — without warning — it felt impossible," his family said.

The Family's Deepest Pain
— A Loss Too Great to Bear

His wife and children, who had waited for him through every danger, now faced the storm they could never prepare for — life without him.

"He was our anchor. The one who always came home. And now, suddenly, he was gone," Eleni said.

The man who had stood strong for everyone else was now gone in silence, leaving a void that could never be filled.

Five Years Later
— A Memorial in a Nation's Grieving Heart

On August 28, 2023, five years after Christos' passing, his family gathered to hold his memorial, remembering a life of love, strength, and sacrifice.

But this day carried a double weight of mourning, because it was also the six-month memorial of Greece's most devastating train accident in a hundred years — the Tempi railway tragedy that claimed the lives of so many young people on February 28, 2023.

The coincidence was impossible to ignore:

Christos' five-year memorial became intertwined with the memory of the young souls lost in Tempi.

Two tragedies — one personal, one national — sharing a day of tears and remembrance.

As Eleni stood at her father's grave, she thought not only of her own father, but of the many families now grieving their children.

"It was as if the pain of our family met the pain of an entire country that day. We mourned my father, but also all those young people who never made it home — as my father did, so many times before fate took him."

A Nation's Tears
— A Family's Private Loss in a Public Tragedy

That day, as Greece lit candles for the victims of Tempi, Christos' family lit candles for him, and in that moment, the private and public grief became one.

His daughter Eleni reflects:

> *"On that day, I understood that loss is universal. The same way we grieved for our father, now mothers and fathers across Greece were grieving for their children. And I know my father, a man of deep compassion, would have stood with those families, in their pain, as he always stood with those in need."*

A Man of the People, Forever Honored

Even as a private man, Christos Kapatos had always carried others' pain with him:

He fought for his crew in Jeddah.

He carried the weight of his family's pain when he was nearly killed.

He led with empathy, not only with authority.

And in death, his family knew he would be standing in spirit with all those who lost loved ones in Tempi, a captain not just of ships, but of compassion and solidarity.

His Lasting Legacy

Today, Christos' name is still spoken with respect, not only as a Master Captain but as a man of extraordinary honor and humanity.

His daughter Eleni still carries his lessons in her heart:

> *"He taught me that real strength is quiet, that love means sacrifice, and that we must always protect those who depend on us — even when no one else will."*

His grandchildren grow up hearing the stories — of the captain who sailed through storms, who brought his men home, and who loved his family beyond life itself.

Final Reflection
— A Light That Guides, Even in the Darkest Sea

Though Christos Kapatos' life ended on a day of tragedy, his story continues to guide those he left behind.

His life teaches us that:

Even when life ends, love endures.

Even when we are lost in the storm, his example shows us how to navigate home.

Even when grief breaks us, his lessons give us the strength to stand again.

"A man of honor never truly dies. His life becomes a lighthouse that guides others through the darkest seas."

In Loving Memory of Christos Kapatos
(Born August 15, 1964 – Passed away August 28, 2018)
"A life of dignity, love, and sacrifice — remembered forever."

Final Words to Readers

T o all who read this story:

May you carry with you the lessons of Christos Kapatos — to live with honor, to love deeply, and to never abandon those who depend on you.

And may his memory be a reminder that even in a world of tragedy, there are people who show us what it means to be truly human — strong, kind, and full of quiet courage.

As I finish writing these words, I find myself sitting in silence, thinking of my father.

Writing this book has been one of the most emotional journeys of my life — because in telling his story, I have had to walk through the storms he endured, the sacrifices he made, and the love he carried for all of us, even when it cost him everything.

My father, Christos Kapatos, was not a man who sought recognition. He never asked to be called a hero.
To him, being strong for others, protecting his family, standing by his crew, and doing what was right — those were simply part of who he was.

But I believe that stories like his must be told.

Because in a world where we often forget the quiet heroes, the men and women who live with honor when no one is watching, we need to be reminded of what true courage and love look like.

I wrote this book not only for him, but for everyone who has loved and lost someone who lived with dignity, strength, and sacrifice. I wrote this for the children who want to remember their parents' stories, and for the parents who silently carry their families through life's storms without asking for anything in return.

My dearest FATHER I am giving you this book, a 'unique journey" through time' to express my feelings, my thoughts, my grief - maybe my sadness looks very similar to anger, and both are really about disappointment and grief - to remind you of the beautiful moments we had, and the most important to tell you how much I loved and I love you. How much I need you. Father, you were my rock. You were always there to catch me when my knees buckle. There are no words to express how grateful I am to you. Father, for everything you have given to me. Your dedication and sacrifice are the reasons I have such beautiful life. I could never give back half of what you have given me over the course of your years. Please know that I appreciate you each and every day.

Today I recognize you, FATHER, for all that you are and all that you do. I feel so fortunate to have been raised by a real SUPERHERO. Today, I want to let you know that you are deeply loved and appreciated.

Father, you deserve the world today. You are the most generous, kind, and thoughtful dad a kid could ever ask for.

Thank you, Father, for always putting me first, never being short on time or patience, and making me feel loved. Father, we have battled some stormy seas, but together we overcome all the difficulties and all the challenges.

"On this memory book" pages I made drawings, I wrote you messages full of respect and love, stuck photos and magically traveled back in time because I was constantly thinking of you, the best dad in the world.

You were a man of honor dad, because in such adverse circumstances that you grew up as a child, you successfully managed this difficult life and became successful, wiseful and respectable.

Brave, Yes, because you were an orphan from the age of 8 and a hard worker from that age. You had awards and honours at sports, an accomplished athlete and you gained school certification with distinctions marks. Your favourite lesson was being "Plato's Logic". How many times while coming home did I heard the CD playing from downstairs, listening to Cavafy's poetry set to music. The collection that had been published in a newspaper. Which I have as a memory collection to treasure for ever. Our memories mold how we develop, how we think, and "who" we become as well as how we change.

You graduated with distinctive marks from the "Merchant Navy Academy of Hydra" as "Master A" and having Second university studies in Melbourne, Australia, you differentiate yourself and built a standout career that everyone admired. How many people did I met in shipping industry from your neighbourhood and all saying to me "We had your father as a "role-model", we grew up with him".

HERO, My Beloved Father, because the time I was born just a few days after, you were stabbed to death, in front of your father's house.

Hero, My Beloved Father, because you stayed alive and didn't leave me an orphan without having met such a great person. A very logical and emotional character, a very rare combination. And a mother which did not go through the teenage stage but became suddenly an adult and later a rock for the family.

Hero because you were "Very Proud" like the heroes of revolution at Messolonghi and strong like the mountain Ainos, of Kefalonia. Insightful and a man with spirit, with values and ideals, fair and wise.

"In the bible, from the beginning, we know the role that our God has given to a father.

Dearest DAD, My DAD you have been the biggest influence in my life. A father is he who guides his Only daughter through life, and now even in death you guide me.

You are constantly show me that love never dies. You speak to me through music and if I listen carefully I can still hear your kind and soulful voice like when you were singing to us, remember?

Father, When you died my grief became so overwhelming and suffocating that on numerous occasions I was convinced that I too was dying. My heart was so heavy and the pain was unbearable when I lost you. You keep showing me that love never dies. You played a major role in my life and now you were gone. So many years of being a "Daddy's girl" And now just like that you were gone.

"The people who I thought were going to be my anchors quickly became the holes in my lifeboat."

Complete, utter disappointments. I was desperately needed kindness, love and support, anything else seemed cruel and unwelcome. Taking a page out of your book I chose to break ties and ignore. One of the greatest lessons you taught me is to quiet a fool with silence. Unfortunately death brings out quite a few fools.

"But you prepared me for this."

From teaching me how to walk, to throw a ball, even to dance while standing on top of your feet, you showed me ways to stand on my own two feet. A dad's job is not only to protect his little girl, but also to show her how to defend herself when, «one day», he is not around.

Father, Your death has been a *"mysterious"* doorway with so much painful grieving for me. Heartache that I never knew was possible and mysterious because I never know how or when that door is going to open and pull me in.

I remember, when I'm driving to work in the morning and for a moment I can feel you sitting next to me in the car. Or when a beautiful fluffy white feather crosses my path, and I smile because I know it's you sending me love from above.

Not now but from my childhood I have found enough feathers to build my own angel wings and visit you in Heaven.

I prayed and begged God to protect you. At the end of your life I was so angry that my prayers were not answered. You were not supposed to die; it seemed like such a cruel death sentence for such a great man. Angry with those that caused it but still a "Brave", Young's" man death.

To you, dear reader, I want to say this:

As I wrote these pages, I was flooded with memories:

Of his strong hands holding mine when I was small.

Of his quiet voice reading poetry — Kavafis echoing through our home, teaching me to see life as a journey full of meaning and beauty.

Of the way he looked at us — with eyes that said everything he never put into words.

Of his deep sense of responsibility, always putting others first.

And, as I wrote, I cried for all the things I wish I could still say to him. But through these pages, I have found a way to speak to him again, to honor him, and to share him with the world.

If you have ever had someone in your life — a father, a mother, a mentor, a friend — who gave you everything they had, even when they had little left for themselves,
If you have ever loved someone who stood strong so that you could grow,
If you have ever watched someone live with integrity even when life was unfair —

Then you already know my father.

Because my father lived for love.
He lived for family.
He lived for honor.

And I hope that in reading his story, you carry a piece of him with you, too — as I do, every day.

So now, I leave you with this final message, the heart of everything my father taught me:

> "*Life will bring you storms. But sail them with honor.*
> *Love deeply, even when it hurts.*
> *Stand strong for those who need you.*
> *And always, always come home to those you love.*"

Thank you, from my heart, for reading his story.

Thank you for letting me share him with you.

If you carry a piece of him with you as you close this book, then his life — and his love — will continue to sail on.

Thank you for walking this journey with me, for remembering him, and for honoring the quiet strength that so many live by and yet so few speak of.

If you are facing storms of your own, I leave you with something my father taught me — words that guided him across every ocean and through every hardship:

"The sea is never without storms — but if you stay true to your course and hold steady to what is right, you will always find your way home."

With all my heart,

Elen Kapatou

"Sail on, Captain. You are forever in our hearts."

"In memory of my father,
Christos Kapatos — A Man of Honor, A Man of Love."

www.ingramcontent.com/pod-product-compliance
Lightning Source LLC
Chambersburg PA
CBHW031228120626
46545CB00003B/1039